BOONE COUNTY LIBRARY

2040 910 813 242 6

Caring for your scooter

How to maintain & service your 49cc to 125cc twist & go scooter

Trevor Fry

D1117827

WITHDRAWN

BOONE COUNTY PUBLIC LIBRARY
BURLINGTON, KY 41005
www.bcpl.org

OCT 27 2011

Also from Veloce Publishing –
Caring for your car – How to maintain & service your car (Fry)
Caring for your car's bodywork and interior (Sahota)
Electric Cars – The Future is Now! (Linde)
How your car works – Your guide to the components & systems of modern cars,
   including hybrid & electric vehicles (Linde)
Roads with a View – England's greatest views and how to find them by road
   (Corfield)
Roads With a View – Scotland's greatest views and how to find them by road
   (Corfield)
Roads With a View – Wales' greatest views and how to find them by road (Corfield)
The Efficient Driver's Handbook – Your guide to fuel efficient driving techniques and
   car choice (Moss)
Walking the dog – Motorway walks for drivers and dogs (Rees)

www.rac.co.uk
www.veloce.co.uk

This publication has been produced on behalf of RAC by Veloce Publishing Ltd.
The views and the opinions expressed by the author are entirely his own, and do
not necessarily reflect those of RAC.

First published in July 2011 by Veloce Publishing Limited, Veloce House,
Parkway Farm Business Park, Middle Farm Way, Poundbury, Dorchester, Dorset,
DT1 3AR, England. ISBN: 978-1-845840-95-2 UPC: 6-36847-04095-6

Fax 01305 250479/e-mail info@veloce.co.uk
web www.veloce.co.uk or www.velocebooks.com.

© Trevor Fry and Veloce Publishing 2011. All rights reserved. With the exception of quoting brief passages for
the purpose of review, no part of this publication may be recorded, reproduced or transmitted by any means,
including photocopying, without the written permission of Veloce Publishing Ltd. Throughout this book logos,
model names and designations, etc, have been used for the purposes of identification, illustration and decoration.
Such names are the property of the trademark holder as this is not an official publication.
Made under licence from RAC Motoring Services. The RAC logo is the registered trade mark of RAC Motoring
Services.
Readers with ideas for automotive books, or books on other transport or related hobby subjects, are invited to
write to the editorial director of Veloce Publishing at the above address.
British Library Cataloguing in Publication Data – A catalogue record for this book is available from the British
Library.
Typesetting, design and page make-up all by Veloce Publishing Ltd on Apple Mac.
Printed in India by Replika Press.

Caring for your scooter

How to maintain & service your 49cc to 125cc twist & go scooter

Trevor Fry

Contents

Introduction

Who is this book for?

This book is for anyone who wants to maintain their 49cc to 125cc 'twist & go' scooter and gain a little knowledge, and a great deal of satisfaction, at the same time.

Somebody who doesn't want to spend time wading through a highly technical manual – probably getting lost in the process – just to find out how to adjust the rear brake!

Why buy this book?

It's written in plain English and illustrated with full colour photographs. It does not assume you have any mechanical knowledge.

The work is carried out with the most basic of tool sets, and not only will you have the satisfaction of doing the job yourself, but you'll have learnt something along the way.

It will save you money.

This book is not a full-blown, 'take-off every nut and bolt' manual. It covers the basic servicing and maintenance needed to keep your scooter safe and on the road.

What's covered

Fluids
Brakes
Filters
Tyres
Lights
Sparkplug
Electrics
Cables
Cleaning the scooter
Safety checks

What's not covered

Older scooters with manually-operated clutch and gear selection
Total engine rebuild
Total gearbox rebuild
Carburettor rebuild
Removal of speed restriction/power output
Bearing replacement

Important information

Make/model	
Registration	
Engine number	
Oil type/capacity	
Sparkplug number	
Tyre size/pressures	
Front	
Rear	

Safety

● If anything contained in this handbook contradicts what's written in the official user's handbook that came with your scooter, the user's handbook will *always* take priority.

● Sometimes in our photos some of the body panels of our project scooter have been removed to allow you to see more easily see what's happening. Unless instructed otherwise, these panels do not need to be removed for you to perform the same job.

● This handbook is not model specific, but, whilst your scooter and its individual components may look a little different from our project scooters and their components, the jobs described will still be performed in essentially the same manner.

● When doing any maintenance always turn off the engine and remove the ignition key.

● All bolts, nuts and screws are turned **anti-clockwise to undo,** unless stated otherwise in the user's handbook.

● Dust from brake shoes and pads can be harmful to health, so wear a face mask when working on the brakes. It's a good idea to clean the brake assemblies with a proprietary brake cleaner or rinse them out with clean water, to keep the dust down.

● Always use the correct size tools (spanners, sockets, screwdrivers, etc) or you risk rounding off nuts and the heads of bolts, or stripping the slots out of screws. Also, you increase the risk of injuring yourself if the tool slips when you're applying pressure.

Daily before you ride

Check lights
Note: Some scooters require that the engine is running in order for you to check all lights.

All lights should be in working order:

Headlight high beam and low beam.
Is the headlight reflector clean.
Riding light (if fitted).
Rear light.
Brake light. (Brake light operation can be checked by backing up to a garage door or other partly reflective surface. Check that both the front and rear brake levers operate the brake/stop light.)
Indicator (turn signal) lights.

Check brakes
Check brake fluid level if your scooter has an hydraulic brake (usually the case for scooters with a front disc brake). See chapter 1 section A3.

Pull on the front brake lever: the scooter shouldn't move forwards when fully applied. The lever should not require more than one half of its potential total movement before the brake is fully applied.
Pull on the rear brake lever or press on the pedal: the scooter shouldn't move forwards when fully applied. The lever or pedal should not require more than one half of it potential total movement before the brake is fully applied.

Brakes shouldn't make a grinding sound when in use (indicating worn out brake pads/shoes).

Check engine oil level
See chapter 1 section A2. Check oil level, via the level window or by using the dipstick. Note that these items may not be present on a water-cooled two-stroke scooter.

If the oil level is low, then top up. If there's an oil leakage, find the source of the leak and repair before riding the scooter.

Check tyres
See chapter 1 secton J.
If a tyre is flat or partially deflated, inflate it to the correct pressure and recheck the pressure after 30 minutes. If it's still losing pressure, get the tyre checked and repaired as necessary at a tyre and exhaust centre.

If the tyre tread is worn down level with any of the minimum depth indicators or has damaged walls, cuts, bulges, etc, renew it.

Check coolant level
Most scooters will **not** have a coolant tank, check your owner's handbook to find out if yours has. If fitted, the coolant tank can be in one of two places: within the leg shield (under the handlebars) or under the seat. **Caution!** do not attempt

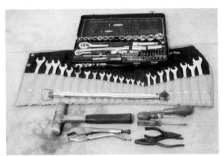

Fig 2. A good range of tools is essential.

Recommended tools

Socket set (4-21mm)
Selection of spanners (6-14mm)
Correct size sparkplug spanner
Torque wrench
Allen keys
Selection of screwdrivers (both flat and crosshead)
Pliers
G-clamp (small)
Insulation tape
Soft-faced mallet
Feeler gauge
Latex gloves
Wire or stiff bristle brush
A selection of graded 'wet and dry' abrasive papers

Fig 1. A coolant reservoir located under the handlebars.

to check coolant level when the engine is hot, there is a risk of scalding.

To check the level, remove the filler cap and look in; there's not normally a dipstick or coolant level gauge. If high coolant temperature is indicated on the temperature gauge, it can be an indication of low coolant level.

Check fuel oil level
If your scooter uses a two-stroke oil/fuel mixture, which you physically mix in the fuel tank, then this doesn't apply to you. However, if the oil and fuel are mixed automatically in the carburetor, then you'll have a separate two-stroke oil tank (most likely under the seat). Undo the filler cap and check the level inside (there's usually no other way of determining the level).

Piece of card
Large piece of card to push screws/bolts into. You can then label them all and record their position so you can put them back exactly where they came from; it will also prevent them getting lost.

Mobile phone with camera/digital camera
Taking pictures of an assembly before and during dismantling will help during reassembly, if you find yourself in doubt about how it all goes back together correctly.

one
Maintenance

SECTION A: Fluids

1: Oils/filters – change intervals
The following intervals are given as a guide only. Refer to your scooter handbook for manufacturer's recommended intervals.

Engine oil – change every 600 miles (1000km)
Transmission oil – change every 3000 (5000km)
Air filter – clean every 1000 miles and change every year
Oil filter – clean every oil change. If your scooter has a foam filter, it should be changed every year or 2000 miles
Brake fluid – change every two years

Caution! Oils and brake fluids can irritate eyes and skin, so wear safety glasses and latex gloves (or use a barrier cream) when working with them.

2: Checking/topping up/changing engine oil and oil filter
If your scooter has a two-stroke, water-cooled engine, this section may not apply to you, but you'll still need to follow the sections on coolant and transmission oil.

Engine oil top up
Required:
New engine oil
Cloth or tissue
Funnel

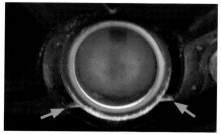

Fig 3. Typical engine oil level window (note: minimum level marker).

Working on a level surface and with the engine cold, place the scooter on its centre stand (if fitted), otherwise get a helper to hold the scooter upright. If the scooter is not level the oil level reading will be incorrect.

If the engine has just been running, wait 5 minutes for the oil to settle to the bottom of the engine.

If the scooter has an engine oil level window – this will be set into the side of the engine, near to the bottom – use it to check the oil level Fig 3.

The oil level needs to be at, or just below, the upper level marker.

If the crankcase has no window, then the oil level check is performed via a dipstick fitted on the end of the engine oil filler plug (Fig 4).

Clean the crankcase filler plug

Fig 4. Typical position of oil filler plug/ dipstick.

Fig 5. Typical dipstick.

Fig 6. Dipstick oil level marker zone.

and surrounding area with a tissue to prevent dirt falling into the crankcase when the plug is removed.

Unscrew the plug and wipe the whole of the dipstick with a clean tissue or cloth.

You may see that there are upper and lower level markers, as in Fig 6 – the upper level is where the 'XXXX' area begins and the lower level is where it ends – or your scooter's dipstick may just have straightforward marks for maximum and minimum.

If you didn't wipe the dipstick before putting it back in the crankcase you'll get a false reading, because oil is splashed over the dipstick while the engine is running.

Put the plug back into the crankcase, but don't screw it in (unless instructed to do so by the user's manual), and then remove it again. You should now be able to see the level of the oil on the markers.

If the oil level is halfway between the markers or lower, ie, towards the lower level marker, or you cannot see any oil at all, then add oil as required via the crankcase filler hole, using a funnel if necessary.

If you can't see oil in the window, or if the oil level is below the lower marker, don't run the engine until the cause of the low oil level is known and the situation remedied.

When topping up add oil slowly, repeatedly checking the level, until the required level is reached.

Note: Too much oil can cause as much damage to the engine as too little.

Replace the crankcase filler plug, but **don't** over-tighten; finger-tight is enough.

Ride the scooter for about ten minutes, and then recheck the oil level once the engine has cooled. Top up with more oil if needed.

Check for leaks.

Oil change/oil filter change

Required:
Socket set
New oil (grade and quantity as specified in the user's handbook)
New filter (if being changed)
Cloth/tissue
Container to collect old oil in
Funnel
A small mirror (helpful if you can't see the drain plug)
Rubber/latex gloves (you will get oil on your hands)
Copper washer for drain plug (if fitted)

Run the scooter so that the engine is warm. The engine should be warm enough so that you can touch it in the immediate vicinity of the drain plug without burning yourself. **Caution!** If the engine is excessively hot, wait for it to cool a little, otherwise you risk being burnt by the hot oil as it runs out.

Fig 8. Typical crankcase oil drain plug (arrowed). Clean the whole area before removing.

Warming the engine helps the oil to flow more easily.

Turn off the engine and remove the ignition key. Wait five minutes for the oil to settle in the bottom of the engine.

Working on a level surface, place the scooter on its centre stand (if fitted), otherwise get a helper to hold the scooter upright: if the scooter is not level, all the old oil may not be able to drain out.

Find the oil drain plug on the underside of the engine (Fig 8). You can use a small mirror to help locate the drain plug beneath the engine.

In most cases the drain plug is on the right (as you sit on the scooter), just behind the exhaust pipe.

Clean the plug and surrounding area with a stiff brush.

Locate the correct size socket head to fit the oil drain plug, and undo

Fig 7. Typical location of engine oil drain plug (arrowed).

Fig 9. Close-up of a typical oil drain plug with a collar (arrowed) for a sealing ring.

the plug fractionally (so you're sure you have the correct size socket). The plug can be tight due to the constant changes of temperature it endures, so be sure to use the correct size socket to avoid damaging it should your socket slip. The drain plug may be no more then a standard-looking bolt with a copper washer fitted, or, as shown in Fig 9, may have a collar on which a rubber, fibre or copper sealing ring may be seated.

Place a suitable container on the ground beneath the plug to catch the draining oil. Loosen the drain plug using the socket spanner, and then undo it completely with your fingers (so you can keep hold of the plug and stop it falling into the oil container). There will usually be a spring above the plug that holds the oil filter in place; this does not need to be removed unless you intend to change or clean the filter.

To change the oil filter, pull out this spring (if it does not fall out anyway) by either hooking it with the end of your finger or with a small screwdriver: it shouldn't be very tight. Note which way up the spring fits, as it'll need to be refitted in the same fashion.

With the drain plug fully removed, clean the area around the crankcase filler plug and remove it; this will allow air to enter the crankcase to aid oil drainage.

Leave the oil to drain for at least 10-15 minutes, to allow as much of the old oil to escape as possible.

Wipe and examine the drain plug for damage, replace the copper washer (or examine the rubber seal for damage, and replace if necessary).

When draining has finished, wipe around the drain hole, replace the filter (if removed), reinsert the spring (with a slight rotating motion, making sure it's the correct way up); then replace the drain plug and tighten. (Refer to chapter 4 for torque settings.)

Fig 10. Oil draining.

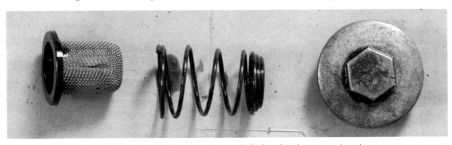

Fig 11. Typical oil filter, spring and drain plug in correct order.

If your oil filter is of the wire mesh type, as in Fig 11, then, when doing an oil change, examine the filter for corrosion. If you have a foam filter, examine it for tears and replace if necessary, or, in any case, after 2000 miles. To clean a foam filter, rinse it in fresh engine oil.

Refill the engine with the correct grade and quantity of oil, using a funnel and checking the oil level as you go. **Do not** over-fill.

Replace the engine oil filler plug, but **do not** over-tighten; finger-tight is enough.

Ride the scooter for about ten minutes and recheck the oil level after allowing the engine to cool; top up if required.

Check for leaks.

Dispose of the old oil in an environmentally responsible manner. Your local recycling centre will have suitable facilities.

3: Hydraulic brakes/brake fluid
Checking operation & topping up
Required:
Brake fluid (DOT4-type)
Spanner
Screwdriver

Checking operation
Because the wear of the brake pads and discs is compensated for

Fig 13. Another typical reservoir side window.

automatically, no adjustment will ever be necessary. If, however, the brake lever operation begins to feel 'soft/spongy,' or braking appears to be less effective, and the brake pads are not excessively worn, this could indicate air/moisture in the hydraulic system which will require the brakes to be bled (see next section), or a low hydraulic fluid level indicating the need for a top up.

Topping up brake fluid
Note: When topping up or changing the hydraulic brake fluid, you should only ever use DOT4-standard brake fluid. Check the label on the bottle.

The brake fluid for the front brake can be checked by examining the fluid level window (if there is no window, the reservoir needs to be opened to see the fluid level). The fluid level window is normally in one of two positions on the reservoir: see Figs 12 and 13. The reservoir is usually part of the front brake lever assembly. It may be necessary to remove the handlebar cowling (normally held in place by screws or bolts on the underside) to see the fluid level.

Fig 12. Typical brake fluid reservoir side window.

Fig 14. Reservoir top cover plate.

Fig 16. Rubber diaphragm.

Fig 15. Plastic seal (may not be fitted).

Fig 17. Topping up brake fluid.

Ensure the reservoir is horizontal so the reading is accurate. There may be maximum and minimum markers in the window (refer to the scooter's handbook). If the window has no markers then the window itself is used, in that the top of the window is the maximum fluid level and the bottom is the minimum fluid level.

In Fig 12 we can see that it's possible to check the reservoir level without removing the handlebar cowling.

In Fig 13 we've had to remove the handlebar cowling to see the fluid level.

If the brake fluid isn't clear, light gold, or bronze in colour, but dark brown or black, then renew it by bleeding (see next section).

If the brake fluid is clean but near the low level mark, top it up. Wipe the top cover plate with a clean cloth to stop dirt or grit getting into the reservoir. **Caution!** It's imperative that you don't introduce dirt/grit into the reservoir, as this will cause damage to internal components of the hydrailic braking system and affect braking performance.

Note: Cover all paintwork in the vicinity of the reservoir, as, if dripped, brake fluid will discolour/damage it.

Remove the screws securing the top cover plate and lift it from the reservoir (Fig 14), remove the plastic seal, if fitted (Fig 15), and then carefully remove the rubber diaphragm (Fig 16), noting which way round it's fitted. **Note:** if the rubber diaphragm appears perished or cracked, renew it.

Do not operate the brake lever with the reservoir top cover plate removed (doing so may cause brake fluid to spill out of the reservoir, and/or allow air into the system).

Fill the reservoir to the required level using new brake fluid. **Caution!** Do not re-use old brake fluid. Brake fluid is hygroscopic and will absorb moisture from the atmosphere, which, in turn, will cause a deterioration in braking power.

After topping up to the required level, replace the rubber diaphragm, making sure it's the correct way round and seated correctly. Refit the plastic seal, ensuring it's correctly seated, and refit the top cover plate, making sure it, too, is installed correctly and tight.

Operate the brake a few times and check for leaks (pay particular attention around the join between the top cover plate and the brake fluid reservoir) before going for a ride. Be particularly cautious on the test ride, until you're sure the brakes are working properly and reliably.

Changing brake fluid (bleeding the brake)
Required:
Brake fluid (DOT4-type)
Screwdriver
Spanner
Plastic bleed tube
Jar

Check that the brake fluid level is at

Fig 18. Bleed valve (always at top of calliper), arrowed. Note dust cap.

Fig 19. Bleed valve, tube and jar set up.

maximum. If not, top up as required (see previous section).

Fit the correct size ring spanner on the bleed valve on the brake calliper, having first cleaned the valve nipple. Attach a tight-fitting piece of plastic tubing to the bleed valve nipple. Place the other end of the tube into a clean glass or plastic container – a small glass jar or similar (Fig 19).

Pour some fresh brake fluid into the container, until the end of the tube is covered by about 2cm (¾in) of fluid. Note that the end of the tube must remain immersed at all times during bleeding.

With the bleed valve in the closed

position, apply pressure to the system using the brake lever by pulling it on two or three times, and then hold it in the 'on' position. With the brake lever still held on, partially open the bleed valve to allow brake fluid to be expelled into the plastic tube. As this happens you will feel the brake lever move toward the handlebar. As the lever approaches the end of its travel, close the bleed valve. Then release the brake lever.

Note: The bleed valve should be loosened only slightly in order for brake fluid to be expelled when under pressure. **Do not** fully remove the bleed valve!

Check the fluid level in the brake reservoir, topping up with fresh brake fluid as necessary.

Repeat this process until the brake fluid coming out of the tube is clean and contains no air bubbles.

When finished, check the brake fluid level in the reservoir.

Ensure that the bleed valve is closed. Take particular care not to over-tighten the bleed valve: it's very easy to strip the thread or break off the nipple, leaving the threaded part in the caliper body! Check that the reservoir cover is correctly refitted. Check for leaks around the reservoir top and bleed valve.

Pump the brake lever to ensure it's working correctly. If its action feels soft, or 'spongy,' there may be air in the system. In this case continue to bleed the brake system as before, checking for air bubbles coming out of the tube.

Dispose of the used brake fluid as it cannot be used again. Your local recycling centre will have the correct disposal facilities.

4: Transmission oil (may also be described as gear oil or final drive oil)
Required:

New oil (grade and quantity as specified in the scooter's handbook)
Spanners
Socket set
Container to collect old oil in

Transmission oil is used to lubricate the gears and the final drive shaft in the rear hub. On most scooters the oil can be changed without having to remove the transmission belt cover.

With the scooter on its centre stand locate both the filler plug and the drain plug. The drain plug will be on the underside of the transmission case at the lowest point, while the level plug will be on the side or end of the case in a somewhat higher position.

The amount of oil required may be marked on either the front or rear of the transmission cover. Most scooters take about 0.12 litres (4.22 fl oz), but check the scooter's handbook.

To change the oil, put a container under the drain plug and remove it, having first cleaned the plug and its surrounding area. Wear latex gloves to prevent the oil coming into contact with your skin.

Remove the filler plug to allow air to enter the transmission case and aid oil drainage. Leave the oil to drain for at least 15 minutes, or as long as possible. Replace the drain plug and add the correct amount of oil via the filler hole. The filler hole is also the oil level

Fig 20. Rear of a typical transmission case.

Fig 21. Transmission filler/level plug (arrowed).

Fig 22. Transmission drain plug (arrowed).

indicator, so when oil flows back out of the filler hole the oil level is correct.

5: Coolant (water-cooled scooters)
Checking and topping up
Required:
Water and anti-freeze (proportions of each will be found in the anti-freeze instructions)

Caution! Do not attempt to check or top up the engine coolant while the engine is hot; there's a serious risk of scalding.

The coolant tank will be either contained within the leg shield (under the handlebars), or under the seat. If the scooter has a coolant level dipstick, it will have maximum and minimum level markers. Alternatively, the levels may be marked on the reservoir itself. With some scooters there is no means of measurement, and if that's the case with yours, you'll need to watch the temperature gauge in the main panel carefully, and top up the coolant if the scooter starts running hot.

Don't over-fill when topping up the coolant tank.

Failure to maintain the correct coolant level can cause the engine to run at temperatures which exceed its safe working limit, resulting in serious damage.

Fig 23. Coolant reservoir filler cap (DO NOT open when HOT!)

SECTION B: Brakes

1: How brakes work
Drum brakes (front and rear, lever-operated)

When the brake lever is operated, the brake cable pulls the brake arm assembly on the side of the hub. This movement is transferred into the brake drum via a spindle that carries a cam which sits between the brake shoe ends. When the spindle turns, its cam pushes the brake shoes outward, causing the shoes to bind against the inside of the drum, thereby producing the braking effect. On releasing the lever, springs attached to the brake shoes pull them back in, away from the drum.

Drum brakes (rear, pedal-operated)

When the brake pedal is pushed, a rod or cable running from the pedal actuates the rear brake arm assembly on the outside of the hub. The brake shoes then operate and release in the same way as the lever-operated items. In the case of the rod mechanism, there may be a supplementary spring sited under the pedal. The drum set up is the same as for the lever-operated brake.

Disc brakes

Pulling the brake lever, or depressing the brake pedal on a rear hydraulically-operated brake, pushes a piston in the brake master cylinder (usually combined with the fluid reservoir/brake lever or pedal assembly). The piston, in turn, pushes hydraulic fluid down the feed pipe and into the brake calliper which sits over the brake disc. The pressurised brake fluid pushes against a piston in the body of the calliper, forcing the piston to move outward which movement pushes the brake pads against the brake disc, causing the braking effect. On releasing the

Fig 24. Typical front drum brake.

Fig 25. Typical front disc brake.

brake lever/pedal, hydraulic pressure is reduced and the brakes are released.

Note: disc brakes do not completely release from the brake disc, as brake shoes do.

Determine the type of brakes your scooter has

If there's a disc on one or both sides of the wheel then you have an hydraulic brake on this wheel.

If there's a lever actuator on the side of the wheel attached to a cable or rod, then you have a drum brake on this wheel.

Scooters can have disc brakes on both wheels, a disc brake on the front and a drum brake on the rear, or drum brakes on both wheels.

2: Adjusting non-hydraulic brakes
Required:
Pliers
Spanner

As time goes by, the brake cable/s will stretch and the brake shoes will wear so, at some point, the brakes will need to be adjusted to compensate.

This is accomplished via the cable adjusters (if fitted) sited at the point where the brake cable enters the brake lever assembly. However, it is more likely that the adjuster/s will be at the wheel end of the brake cable/s, sited at the point where the brake cable is attached to the brake actuating arm/s in the wheel hub/s.

Adjustment at lever end of the brake cable
Note: Minor adjustments are carried out via the brake lever adjusters (if fitted), whereas larger adjustments are carried out at the wheels.

If the scooter has brake adjusters at the brake lever end of the cable, you'll see that where the cable exits the lever assembly, it passes through a threaded tube that has a large locking collar on it.

To adjust the cable, loosen the locking collar, then unscrew the threaded tube (screw it outward) to tighten the cable. You need to adjust the cable so that the lever travels about 13mm (½in) before the brake comes on. You can check this by pushing the scooter forward and applying the brake. Once you have correctly adjusted the lever, tighten the locking collar.

If there is still too much movement at the brake lever when the threaded tube is in its outermost position, adjust the threaded tube so that it is screwed halfway into the lever assembly,

Fig 26. If your scooter has adjusters at the lever end of cables, they'll be in the arrowed positions. However, you'll probably have to remove the cover above the handlebars to gain access.

Fig 27. Typical brake (cable) adjuster at handlebar lever end of cable. Scooters which have adjusters at the brake end of the cable (see photos on page 21) will not have one at the lever end. Hydraulically operated brakes will not have adjusters of this type at all. Unscrewing the threaded tube (arrowed) will push the end of the cable sleeve outward and reduce slack movement in the brake lever.

and then lock it with the locking collar. (Be aware that this may have occured because the brake shoes are excessively worn and require renewal.)

Proceed as described in the following section.

Fig 28. Typical front brake actuating arm and adjuster (arrowed).

Fig 29. Typical back brake actuating arm and adjuster (arrowed).

Adjustment at wheel end of the brake cable
Required:
Spanner

With the scooter on its centre stand, adjusting the brake (front or rear) is simply a matter of screwing the nut on the end of the cable (or rod) inward. In effect this shortens the cable. **Do not** over-adjust, though, as this will cause the brake shoes to bind and overheat. The brake lever or pedal should move

approximately 13mm (½in) before the brake begins to operate.

In all cases, if you cannot get the correct adjustment and the brake shoes are in a good condition, then the cable will need to be renewed.

Fitting a new brake cable
To renew the cable, undo the adjuster at the wheel hub, then undo the adjuster at the lever/pedal end, slide the cable nipple out of the brake lever, then remove the old cable and fit the new one. Adjust the new cable as previously described.

3: Replacing brake shoes
Caution! Dust from brake shoes can be harmful if inhaled, so wear a face mask when replacing brake shoes. It's also a good idea to wash the brake drum assembly with clean water before stripping it, to keep the dust down and prevent dirt getting into the drum.

Rear brake shoes
Required:
New brake shoes
Socket set
Spanners
Pliers

In order to get access to the rear brake shoes on some scooters it's advisable to first remove the exhaust system. However, before attempting to remove the exhaust system, soak all fixing nuts and bolts with a proprietary penetrating oil.

First, remove the stud nuts from the exhaust manifold (this is at the engine end of the exhaust system, where it is connected to the engine). Take care when doing this, though, as these nuts will have been subjected to lots of changes in temperature, which makes them tend to rust onto the studs. Because of the position of the manifold,

Fig 32. Driveshaft nut in centre of rear wheel.

Fig 30. Supplementary air feed (spring clip arrowed). Squeeze ears together to loosen.

it's a good idea to support the scooter at an angle to improve access to the manifold stud nuts, but at no more than 45 degrees otherwise engine oil can flow to places it is not supposed to. **Caution!** Breaking a stud may well necessitate removal of the engine and a costly repair, so take care!

Disconnect the supplementary air feed pipe (if fitted) from the exhaust pipe, after releasing the spring clip (Fig 30) by squeezing its ears together.

There are usually two bolts holding the rear, silencer, section of the exhaust system (the fat part): one above the

silencer and one below (often almost hidden behind the exhaust pipe). When these bolts are removed the exhaust can be removed from the scooter. You now have easy access to the driveshaft nut (Fig 32).

The driveshaft nut will be extremely tight, and difficult to remove. Have someone sit on the scooter and hold the rear brake on as tightly as possible; this will stop the wheel moving while you undo the nut.

Release and disconnect the rear brake rod or cable (chapter 1 B2) – this will allow maximum retraction of the brake shoes to ease removal of the wheel.

With the nut removed, pull the

Fig 31. Typical upper and lower exhaust mounting bolts (arrowed).

Fig 33. Exhaust/manifold retaining nuts (arrowed).

Fig 34. Brake shoes in-situ. Note the splines on the driveshaft (arrowed).

Fig 35. Removing or refitting brake shoes.

wheel towards you and off the driveshaft (you may have to tap the wheel with a soft-faced mallet or piece of wood just to get it started). Note that the wheel fits onto splines on the driveshaft (Fig 34).

With the wheel removed you will now have access to the rear brake shoes.

Examine the friction pads on the brake shoes carefully, remembering that it's not unusual for the friction material to wear more at one end of the shoe than the other. The friction material should not be damaged or contaminated, nor should it be less than 2.5mm/0.10in thick. If in any doubt about their condition, renew the brake shoes as a safety precaution.

Using a pair of pliers, remove the bottom spring from the shoes, having noted how it is fitted and taking care not to lose it. It's also possible to remove the shoes without first releasing the springs by turning one shoe out at right angles, away from the back of the drum (Fig 35); but don't trap your fingers!

Whichever approach you take, you should now be able to ease the brake shoes away from their mountings.

Note that the brake shoes are 'handed;' each shoe has one flat end and one curved end. The curved ends fit around the mounting post in the brake assembly, and the flat ends fit against the actuating spindle's cam,

Fig 36. Brake shoes with springs fitted.

Fig 37. Brake shoes (fixed spindle end).

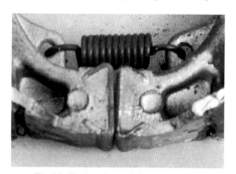

Fig 38. Brake shoes (actuator end).

ie, the spindle that rotates when the brake is applied.

This is a good time to examine the driveshaft and the inside of the brake drum. **Caution!** Do not blow out any brake dust, as it is harmful if inhaled. If there is an excessive amount of brake dust, use a proprietary brake cleaner or wipe it away with a damp cloth. Look for signs of oil leakage close to the driveshaft which could indicate that the driveshaft oil seal needs renewing. **Caution!** Do not ignore this, as oil contamination of the brake shoes will seriously compromise braking performance. Replacement of the driveshaft oil seal is beyond the scope of this book. Take care not to contaminate the brake shoes with oil or grease from your tools or hands.

Fitting the brake shoes is simply the reverse of removal. You can refit them with one spring in position and then, when the shoes are in the correct position, put the other spring in place with a pair of pliers. Alternatively, you can use the right angle method whereby, with the springs fitted, you locate one shoe correctly and then locate the other shoe in position but at right angles (Fig 35), before gently pushing it back into the correct position. This right angle method may be easier as the springs are quite powerful and small, making them difficult to locate correctly with pliers. **Caution!** Whichever method you choose, take care not to trap your fingers!

With the brake shoes back in their correct positions, push the actuating arm to check that both shoes move correctly (only the brake shoe ends around the actuating spindle will actually appear to move).

Before refitting the wheel, check the rear suspension unit for oil leaks from the damper within the spring, and ensure the spring is not broken. Either of these scenarios would mean replacement of the suspension unit; the spring and damper are not repairable, nor can they be separated.

Some scooters have adjustable rear suspension. A special 'C' spanner (normally supplied in the scooter toolkit)

Fig 39. Non-adjustable rear suspension unit.

Fig 40. Adjustable rear suspension unit (adjuster arrowed).

fits onto a collar at the bottom of the rear suspension spring (Fig 40). Turning it will soften or harden the suspension. Bear in mind, though, that altering the preload of the rear suspension will not only affect the smoothness of your ride, but also the braking and handling of the scooter.

While the wheel is off the scooter, take the opportunity to inspect the rear tyre. Look for cuts in the tread and walls of the tyre, bulges in the tyre wall, signs of extreme wear of the tread, or where the canvas inner is showing through; any of which would necessitate the purchase of a new tyre.

When you're satisfied that everything is in good order, you can replace the rear wheel, taking care to align it correctly on the splined shaft. Have someone sit on the machine and apply the rear brake to allow you to tighten the driveshaft nut (refer to chapter 4 for torque settings).

Reconnect the brake rod or cable and adjust the pedal or brake lever so that it travels 13mm (½in) before the brake is applied. Re-adjust if necessary (chapter 1 B2).

Replace the exhaust system, using a new manifold gasket if the exhaust was removed completely. Replace the supplementary air feed pipe (if fitted), and secure it with its spring clip. Double-check everything before riding your scooter.

Caution! New brake shoes will take at least 100 miles to fully bed in, so be aware that the scooter's braking ability will be reduced for a short period of time.

Front brake shoes
Required:
New brake shoes
Socket set
Selection of spanners
Pliers

Screwdriver
G-clamp

Place the scooter on its centre stand on a level surface.

Ensure the scooter is stable and safe, with the front wheel off the ground (most scooters sit with the front wheel off the ground because of the position and weight of the engine).

Disconnect the front brake cable from the wheel by unscrewing the cable adjuster on the brake actuating arm, until there is enough slack to allow you to release the cable outer sleeve from its stop, then the cable nipple from the actuator arm.

Disconnect the speedometer cable from the front wheel hub; it's usually retained by a single screw (Figs 41 & 42). It's a good idea to put a piece of tape over the end of the speedometer cable when it's disconnected, as this will stop the inner cable sliding down through the outer sleeve, and its top end disconnecting from the speedometer itself.

If the speedometer cable fitting is different to that shown here, it's likely that disconnecting it will simply be a

Fig 41. Typical speedometer cable connection.

Fig 42. Speedometer cable disconnected.

Fig 43. Speedometer cable drive unit's component parts.

case of undoing the knurled 'nut' at the cable end from the wheel fitting.

With the brake and speedometer cables disconnected, you can now proceed to remove the wheel. One side of the wheel spindle may have a castle nut with a split pin going through it, or just an ordinary nut. If the spindle is retained by a castle nut, you'll need to straighten the split pin and pull it out of the nut and spindle, using pliers.

With a spanner on one side of the axle and a socket on the other, you can proceed to undo the spindle nut. Note: some scooters with a brake drum on the front wheel also have a 'buffer,' which is a part of the suspension (Fig 44); this does not need to be disconnected to remove the wheel.

With the nut undone you can now remove the spindle.

If you are unable to push the spindle back through the wheel with your fingers, try tapping it with a piece of wood or a soft-faced mallet. **Caution!** Don't use an ordinary hammer, or any other metal object, as this will damage the thread on the end of the spindle. **Caution!** When the spindle has released from one of the forks, the wheel may drop at an angle: make sure your fingers aren't in the way!

Remove the spindle slowly, noting

Fig 45. Brake assembly side of front wheel.

the position of any washers, spacers, and the speedometer drive. There will be a correct position for the brake drum in relation to the suspension leg; also a correct position for the speedometer drive in relation to the wheel, make sure you note these, so they can be

Fig 46. Front wheel spindle removal.

Fig 44. Front suspension 'buffer.'

Fig 47. Although a disc brake model, drum brakes are prevented from rotating by a key like that arrowed.

replaced correctly. It may be a good idea to photograph the assembly with a digital camera/mobile phone before you release the wheel.

When the spindle is out completely, make a note of how the front wheel was set up, ie, the position of any spacers, washers, etc, and from which side the axle was fitted. This is where a piece of cardboard comes in handy because you can lay out and label all the pieces in their correct order ready for reinstallation.

If you haven't yet disconnected the speedometer cable, and the drive assembly is hanging, put a small plastic bag over the end to catch any pieces that may decide to drop out!

If the speedometer drive does come apart, rebuild it immediately and check that it fits to the wheel correctly, so it's ready for when you replace the

wheel. If you look at Fig 43, you'll see that the drive consists of an outer housing, a gear wheel, and a gearbox to transfer the rotation of the wheel to the speedometer dial via the cable. After putting it back together, place a plastic bag over it to stop it coming apart again.

With the wheel free from the front of the scooter, remove it from under the mudguard and lay it on its side with the brake arm assembly uppermost. You can now lift out the wheel hub which holds the whole brake assembly, turn it over, and place it on a piece of board or cloth to prevent it being scratched or damaged on the ground.

Examine and record the layout of the shoes and the springs.

Examine the friction pads on the brake shoes carefully, remembering that it's not unusual for the friction material to wear more at one end of the shoe than the other. The friction material should not be damaged or contaminated, nor should it be less than 2.5mm/0.10in thick. If in any doubt about their condition renew the brake shoes as a safety precaution.

Shoes can be removed by either disconnecting one of the springs using pliers, or by turning one shoe out at right angles to release it from the actuating arm. **Caution!** Take care not to trap your fingers. Replacing the shoes is the reverse of removal. Operate the actuating arm to make sure that the shoes move correctly before refitting the hub assembly to the wheel.

When replacing the front wheel, apply a small amount of multi-purpose grease to the wheel spindle to aid insertion. Make sure the spindle is fitted from the correct side, and that you include any washers/spacers.

Refitting the front wheel is simply a reversal of the steps taken to remove it. Make sure that the speedometer drive and the brake drum are properly seated in relation to both the wheel and the front suspension legs, the brake drum will also have some form of engagement with the forks to stop it rotating.

Tighten the spindle nut (refer to chapter 4 for torque settings), but check you still have free movement of the wheel – it is possible to over-tighten the spindle nut, causing the wheel to bind. Reconnect the speedometer cable (if removed). Reconnect the front brake cable and adjust as required (chapter 1 B2).

4: Checking disc pads
Front and back
Disc pads can usually be checked via a small inspection window in the top or rear of the brake calliper (Fig 48). Remove the rubber bung (if fitted) and, with the aid of a small torch, examine the tops of the pads. You should see the disc in the middle with a brake pad and backing plate on each side.

Fig 48. Calliper brake pad viewing aperture (arrowed).

With some calliper designs, however, it will be easier and quicker to remove the calliper to inspect the pads.

Disc pads have a wear indicator groove (Figs 50 & 55). If they are worn to the extent that the groove has disappeared or is only just visible, the pads must be renewed.

Fig 49. Base of suspension leg, brake calliper and calliper retaining bolts (arrowed).

Fig 50. New and old brake pads. Notice how the friction material has worn down on the old pads. The groove (arrowed) on the new pads indicates the maximum depth to which the pads can be worn before they must be renewed.

Fig 51. Piston (arrowed) partially protruding.

Fig 52. Using an old pad to push the piston back.

5: Replacing disc brake pads

Note: Dust from brake pads and shoes can be harmful if inhaled, so wear a face mask when performing this procedure. It's also a good idea to wash the brake assembly with clean water before stripping it, to keep the dust down.

Front brake

Required:
New brake pads
Socket set

Selection of spanners
Pliers
G-clamp

Caution! Do not operate the brake lever with the calliper disassembled.

To remove the caliper, first place the scooter on its centre stand. Then remove the bolts holding the front brake calliper to the suspension leg (Fig 49). With the bolts removed, you should

Fig 53. Applying pressure with a G-clamp.

Fig 54. Piston pushed fully back and now flush with calliper body.

be able to remove the brake calliper assembly from the brake disc (by pulling it back and turning it to clear the wheel rim). Do not allow the assembly to hang from the brake hose – support it on a block or tie it up.

Looking inside the calliper you'll see that the pads fit into slots.

Remove the pads by allowing them to slide inward in the space normally taken up by the disc. They can be gently eased forward (with the help of a screwdriver, if necessary), taking care not to damage other brake components, such as the brake piston or the rubber seal around the piston.

The brake piston (some scooters have two, but the procedure is the same) will now need to be pushed back into the brake caliper to allow room for the new pads (Figs 52-54).

It's normally possible to do this using an old brake pad and your fingers.

If the piston seems extremely tight, then use a small G-clamp to push it back in (Fig 53), taking care not to damage the alloy outer of the calliper.

Take care not to damage the brake piston or the rubber sealing ring (if fitted). Do not use a hammer to tap the piston back, as the whole assembly is very brittle and could easily crack.

If you can't move the piston, but the calliper and piston appear clean and free of rust/corrosion, pressure can be released from the fluid behind the piston by removing the top of the brake fluid reservoir on the lever assembly on the handlebars. **Caution!** Brake fluid expelled from the reservoir will cause damage to the scooter's paintwork if not protected.

Caution! If there's evidence of severe corrosion on the body of the calliper or on the piston, the caliper will need to be professionally stripped and rebuilt.

Unless absolutely necessary **do not** open the brake fluid reservoir for long periods in damp or wet conditions, as the fluid will draw in moisture from the atmosphere which will cause a deterioration in braking performance.

With the piston back in the correct position, ie, pushed fully back into the calliper, wash your hands (so as not to contaminate the brake pad surfaces with grease or oil); you are now ready to fit new brake pads.

Ensure the brake pads and shims (if fitted) are replaced correctly. Apply

Fig 55. New brake pads correctly fitted in calliper body. Wear indicator grooves arowed.

a thin smear of copper grease to the metal back of the brake pads and shims. **Caution!** Do not contaminate the friction faces of the pads.

Refit the calliper assembly to the front fork. If you find that you have difficulty replacing the calliper because the brake pads move and are preventing you from sliding the caliper over the disc, use a clean pencil, pushed through the inspection aperture, to hold the pads apart: do not use a metal object like a screwdriver as this will damage the brake pad surfaces.

When seated correctly, fit and tighten the calliper retaining bolts, ensuring that they are tightened to the correct torque (see chapter 4).

If you removed it, fit the top back on the brake fluid reservoir.

Double-check everything, and, if all appears correct, pump the front brake lever a few times. This will bring the new pads into contact with the disc. Check that the front wheel rotates fairly freely, bearing in mind that, unlike drum brakes, disc pads are always in contact with the disc, so it will appear as if the brake is dragging slightly. If all is correct then take the scooter for a (careful) test ride.

Caution! New brake pads will take at least 100 miles to fully bed in, so be aware that the scooters braking ability will be reduced for a short period of time.

Rear brakes
Required:
New brake pads

Fig 56. Typical rear disc brake.

Socket set
Selection of spanners
Pliers
G-clamp

Caution! Do not operate the brake lever with the calliper disassembled.

The procedure for replacing the rear brake pads is the same as that for the front brake pads.

SECTION C: Sparkplug

1: Removal, examination, cleaning and refitting
Caution! When doing any maintenance on your scooter, always turn off the engine and remove the ignition key to avoid the risk of electric shock.

Removal
Required:
Screwdriver
Sparkplug spanner
Clean cloth
Feeler gauge
Wire brush or 180 grade wet and dry abrasive paper

Remove the front panel and/or the underseat box.

If you're not able to remove the front panel on its own, the underseat box will have to be removed first.

Normally, there will be four nuts holding the box, and a bolt that attaches it to the front panel.

The front panel is held by screws at the top and bottom. There may also be a screw under the seat, on the inside of the storage box.

Pull the sparkplug cap from the sparkplug; this may be tight as it's a

Fig 57. Front panel/underseat box removed. 1 Rocker cover. 2 Sparkplug cap. 3 Throttle cable. 4 Throttle cable adjuster. 5 Idle speed adjuster. 6 Carburettor. 7 Carburettor jet. 8 Air intake. 9 Fuel pipe. 10 Starter motor relay.

Fig 58. Typical sparkplug connector cap position (arrowed).

Fig 59. Typical sparkplug connector cap.

spring fitting to ensure a good electrical connection. **Note!** Make sure you pull the cap and not the cable!

Using the correctly sized and fully engaged sparkplug socket spanner (they usually have a rubber lining to protect the sparkplug), undo and remove the sparkplug, remembering to turn it anti-clockwise.

Examination

Carefully examine the sparkplug electrode and insulator area closely: its appearance should be similar to the sparkplug examples shown in Figs 61a & 61b.

There should be no damage to the ceramic insulator surrounding the centre electrode. Nor should the area be covered with thick black carbon as in Fig 62 (indicating an over-rich fuel mix).

Oil fouling, as in Fig 63 indicates significant engine wear (accompanied by high engine oil consumption), or a faulty oil/fuel mix on a two-stroke scooter.

Examine the washer attached to the plug thread, this should be undamaged. If you find damage, renew the sparkplug as the washer cannot be removed, and you won't get the good seal with the cylinder head that is needed, leading to a loss of power.

Cleaning
Required:
Wire brush
Cloth

Fig 60. External sparkplug components.

Plug lead connector (some connector caps will not require this connector, in which case it can be unscrewed and removed)

Centre electrode

Insulation recess

Insulator

Insulation nose

Earth (ground) electrode

Fig 61. Normal used sparkplug appearance.
(Courtesy Bosch)

Fig 62. Soot fouling. (Courtesy Bosch)

Clean the electrodes with a cloth to remove oil, and with a wire brush to remove carbon build-up.

Adjust the gap to 0.6mm/0.023in (or to the gap specified in the scooter's handbook) using a feeler gauge. You can buy a special tool to adjust the plug gap, but it can be carefully done using a pair of small, long-nosed pliers to open or close the gap so the feeler gauge fits correctly: it should neither be too loose, nor too tight, just an easy, sliding fit.

Caution! It is possible to check the condition of the spark, but it is not recommended that you attempt this if you're not confident you know what you're doing. Refer to a specialist/ professional.

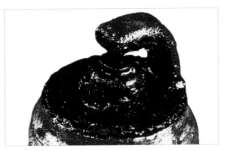

Fig 63. Oil fouling. (Courtesy Bosch)

Refitting
Apply a very small amount of copper grease to the sparkplug thread.

Put the sparkplug into the sparkplug hole and begin screwing it in with your fingers; you may have to put a socket on the sparkplug in order to do this, but, initially, turn the socket head with your fingers only.

The reason for doing this is because the cylinder head into which the plug screws is made from relatively soft aluminum. This makes it extremely easy to cross-thread the sparkplug if any

Fig 64. Check condition of the sealing washer (arrowed).

Fig 65. Refitting sparkplug.

significant force is applied, necessitating an expensive repair.

When you're satisfied the sparkplug is screwing in correctly, tighten with the socket arm, but do not over-tighten (refer to the torque settings in chapter 4). If you're not using a torque wrench, when you feel the sparkplug is fully 'home,' turn the socket arm another 6-7mm (¼in) and no more. Over-tightening will strip the sparkplug thread

from the cylinder head, which will lead to a costly repair!

Replace the plug cap, making sure it's not loose on the sparkplug or on the sparkplug (HT) lead (wire). Also, ensure that there are no sharp kinks in the lead (wire) itself.

Before refitting any panels, it's a good idea to start the engine to ensure you have correctly fitted both the plug and plug lead.

SECTION D: Drivebelt (transmission)

1: Inspection
Required:
New gasket
Socket set
Screwdriver
Spanners

Fig 66. Typical drivebelt/transmission cover (arrowed).

In order for the drivebelt to be inspected the cover needs to be removed. **Note:** On some machines you may have to remove the kickstart pedal, but make a note of the angle and position of the kickstart first (Fig 67), as it will have to be replaced in the same position to correctly start the engine.

Remove the locking bolt and ease the kickstart lever from the spindle. The bolt must be removed fully, as it incorporates a locking mechanism so that, should the bolt come loose, the kickstart lever will not be lost.

Wash the outside of the cover with clean water to prevent dirt falling into the transmission and contaminating the drivebelt or centrifugal clutch mechanism.

Fig 67. Kickstart lever angle is important.

If fitted, remove the air intake pipe from the cover (Fig 68).

Remove the cover, carefully noting which bolt or screw came from which hole (they may be of different lengths), and also the position of any dowels (projecting metal pins) that may be fitted to assist in correct realignment of the cover.

Note: The cover may appear a tight fit because of corrosion on some of the locating dowels.

After ensuring you've removed all the bolts and screws, gently tap off the cover using a rubber or leather mallet (or a piece of wood), taking care not to cause any damage. The cover should now come loose. If a gasket is fitted, and it's in good condition, it may be re-used.

Fig 68. Air intake connection on drivebelt/ transmission cover.

Examine the drivebelt (Fig 70) for signs of extreme wear, particularly on the belt edges, tears or cracks in the belt itself, and missing teeth. In all these

cases the belt will have to be renewed.
Check and grease the teeth on the kickstart mechanism. Apply the grease, then wipe off with a clean cloth, leaving just a thin smear of lubricant.

Check and grease the teeth on the starter motor pinion. Also, ensure that the pinion isn't seized on the spindle. If possible, using a cotton bud, apply a very small amount of grease to the starter pinion shaft.

Check the teeth on the outer edge of the flywheel, and the kickstart connecting lugs in the centre.

If any of the flywheel teeth are severely worn or broken, the flywheel has to be renewed.

Look for signs of oil emanating from behind the flywheel, or from behind the clutch assembly, indicating that an oil seal has failed and needs to be replaced (beyond the scope of this book).

Clean the mating surfaces of the cover and the corresponding edge of the engine case with a soft cloth, onto which WD40, or similar, has been lightly sprayed. **Caution!** Do not allow the cloth to come into contact with the drivebelt, and don't spray directly onto the joint surfaces as you could contaminate the drivebelt.

If all parts are in a satisfactory condition, replace or renew the gasket and refit the cover.

Because the forward end of the starter motor pinion has to engage in a bearing on the inside of the cover, ensure that any dowels in the casing and body line up with their respective holes.

Replace and tighten all bolts/ screws.

Reconnect the air intake pipe and tighten the clip.

Refit the kickstart lever (if removed) ensuring that it's replaced in the same

Fig 69. Behind the cover, the transmission mechanism. 1 starter motor pinion, 2 flywheel (note missing vanes, which means it should be renewed), 3 automatic clutch.

Fig 70. Examine drivebelt carefully for signs of wear or damage.

Fig 72. Check the teeth on the starter motor pinion.

Fig 71. Check and grease the teeth on the kickstart mechanism (inside the drivebelt/transmission cover).

Fig 73. Check the teeth on the outer edge of the flywheel, and the kickstart connecting lugs (arrowed) in the centre for damage.

position it was in before removal, otherwise it may foul on the ground when you attempt to use it (causing not only damage to the arm but also to your ankle!). Ensure the locking bolt is fitted correctly and tightened.

SECTION E: Exhaust

There's not much maintenance you can do in relation to the exhaust system, other than try to keep it as clean as possible. Exhaust systems rust internally due to water content in exhaust gases, volatile changes in temperatures and their exposed position.

If your scooter's exhaust has a removable baffle (there will be a small locking screw at the rear of the exhaust), you can undo this screw and pull out the baffle from inside the silencer. You can then clean the baffle by soaking it in a proprietary cleaner for two or three hours to remove the build-up of carbon, then allow it to dry fully before refitting.

Caution! Any cleaning procedures involving flammable fluids should be done in the open air and well away from any possible source of ignition. Wear protective gloves and protective eyewear.

If you feel the exhaust system is partially blocked by carbon deposits, by far the best solution is to renew it.

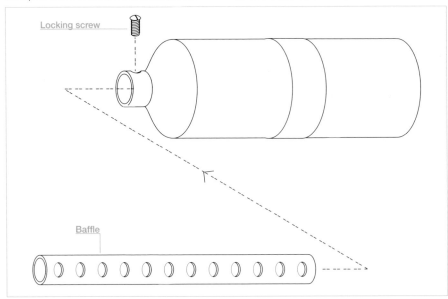

Fig 74. Schematic showing a typical removable baffle. These are rare on modern scooters.

SECTION F: Carburettor adjustments

1: Idle speed adjustment

You may need to do this if your engine runs too fast or too slow when idling.

Required:
Screwdriver

Support the scooter so the rear wheel is off the ground.

Open the viewing panel in the base of the underseat compartment (if fitted); if not, you'll have to remove the box by undoing the (usually) four nuts and the screw attaching the front panel.

This will give you access to the idle screw adjuster and the throttle cable adjuster.

The idle speed is adjusted by turning the throttle adjuster screw (Fig

Fig 76. Typical throttle idle speed adjuster screw.

76), either into or out of its mounting. Turning it inward, will increase engine idle speed and vice versa if you screw it outward. The engine should idle at between 1000-1500rpm (consult the scooter's handbook), and the rear wheel should not be turning (indicating that the idle speed is too high).

Fig 75. Underseat viewing panel open, and we're looking at the top of the carburettor.

Fig 77. Typical throttle cable adjuster at carburettor end.

2: Throttle cable adjustment

You will need to make this adjustment if the throttle twistgrip has to travel too far, or hardly travel at all, before the scooter pulls away.

Required:
Spanners
Pliers

There are two adjusters on the throttle cable: one under the underseat viewing panel, and one under the throttle twistgrip itself – both are secured by locking nuts. The control cable needs to be adjusted so that the throttle doesn't increase engine speed until it has turned at least a 0.6cm (¼in).

Minor adjustments can be carried out at the throttle grip end of the cable. Major adjustment is carried out at the carburettor end of the cable.

Whichever end of the cable you are dealing with, undo the locking nut nearest the end of the cable, then

Fig 78. Typical throttle cable adjuster at throttle twistgrip end.

turn the other nut outward to tighten the cable if there's too much play; or inwards if there's not enough play. Remember to tighten the locking nut when the cable is set correctly.

3: Carburettor jet checking and adjusting

Required:
Screwdriver

The setting and condition of the jet is essential to the correct running of the scooter, as it determines the fuel/air ratio of the mixture fed to the engine.

Locate the jet (normally in the side of the carburettor) and record its current setting by screwing it **into** the carburettor, noting how many turns it takes to fully screw it home (there's no need to tighten it forcefully). Remove the jet, clean it with a cloth, and examine it for wear near the point. If there are signs of excessive wear at the point, then replace it with a new jet.

Return the carburettor to its original setting by screwing the jet fully home, and then unscrewing by the same number of turns as was noted before it was first removed.

Start the engine to check that it accelerates and runs smoothly. If it 'stutters' or 'holds back,' make small adjustments (⅛th of a turn at a time in or out), until it runs smoothly. If you totally lose the correct position, you can always start over.

Fig 79. Carburettor jet adjuster arrowed.

SECTION G: Battery

Required:
Screwdriver
Voltage meter (multimeter)

Caution! Traditional scooter batteries contain acid (often referred to as 'electrolyte'); take great care not to spill the battery contents. Keep battery acid away from hands and eyes. If you do come into contact with battery acid, wash immediately with copious amounts of clean cold water. Medical attention will be required in the event of acid coming into contact with eyes.

Your scooter may use a 6-volt battery or a 12-volt battery; checking and maintenance will be the same for both types.

1: Battery checking, maintenance and charging
Checking

Check your scooter battery's charge and condition at least once a month, otherwise, you could find yourself stranded when least expected.

Turn on the ignition – does the battery light glow steadily (or does the gauge needle move), to show that you have power? If the ignition light is dull or not lit at all, or the meter needle does not move, then it's likely the battery requires attention.

If, when trying to start the engine using the electric starter, the engine turns over slowly, or not at all, it's likely the battery needs charging or renewal.

If the battery is completely discharged ('flat'), you may be able to use the kickstarter (if fitted) to start your scooter. Starting and using your scooter with the kickstart will not be enough to fully charge a flat battery, so it will still require a full charge with a motorcycle battery charger. **Caution!** Don't use a car battery charger to charge your

Fig 80. Typical battery housing. Note the main fuse (arrowed).

scooter's battery – the charge will be too strong and will buckle the battery's internal plates, ruining it!

The battery may be in the underseat compartment or under the foot area.

Check that the power cables are fixed tightly to the terminal heads. A good connection can be helped by applying a small amount of petroleum jelly to the terminal heads after they have been cleaned.

With the ignition turned off and key removed, connect a voltage meter (set to measure DC volts) to the battery (the black lead goes to the (-) negative terminal, and the red lead goes to the (+) positive terminal), taking care not to cause a short circuit.

The voltage shown on the meter should be near to, or just above, the battery voltage, ie, a 12-volt battery may read 11.5-12.6 volts.

To check the condition of the battery you will need to remove it from the scooter.

Ensure the ignition is turned off and the key removed, then undo the battery securing strap (or any securing bracket).

Important! Disconnect the **negative (-)** terminal first, and move the cable away from the battery terminals, then, and only then, disconnect the **positive (+)** terminal.

You can now remove the battery.

Fig 81. Typical sealed battery. Note markings to identify negative (-) and positive (+) terminals.

As you pull it from its location, note the position of the battery breather tube (if fitted), as this needs to go back in the same place.

Maintenance

Caution! Do not attempt to open a sealed battery; no maintenance is necessary other than keeping the connections in good condition and charging when needed. Always keep the battery upright.

If the battery is not of the sealed type, on one side there will be markers to indicate the correct level of electrolyte inside the battery. It will also have removable stoppers in the top, and you'll be able to remove these to top up the battery with **distilled** water.

If the electrolyte level is below the lower marker, the battery needs to be carefully topped-up; do not overfill or use ordinary tap water.

If the battery is showing a low voltage, you may be able to charge it.

Charging

When charging the battery, first ensure that the correct amount of electrolyte is present, and top up if required. Place the battery in a well ventilated area so the fumes from it can disperse during charging; do not attempt to charge the battery whilst it is fitted in your scooter. The charging voltage may seriously damage the entire scooter's electrical system.

Only use a battery charger that is designed to charge a motorcycle battery of the correct voltage; on no

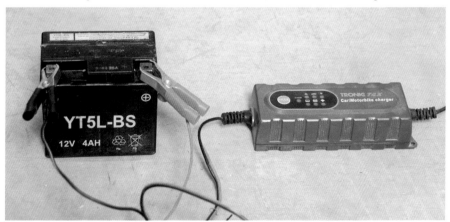

Fig 82. Battery connected to charger. Red cable to '+' terminal, black connector to '-' terminal.

account use a car battery charger as this will destroy the battery plates and render the battery useless.

Do not turn on the charger until it is correctly set to the right voltage and connected to the battery.

Connect the charger's red wire to the (+) positive terminal and the black wire to the (-) negative terminal of the battery.

Pay particular attention to the instructions that came with the battery charger, as it's possible to damage the battery by overcharging it.

When the battery has fully charged, turn off the charger and disconnect the battery.

Refit the battery to the scooter (remembering to push on the breather pipe as it was on removal).

Connect the red wire to the (+) positive terminal first, ensuring the terminal is clean and the cable fixing is tight.

Now connect the black wire to the (-) negative terminal, ensuring the terminal is clean and the cable fixing is tight.

Refit the securing straps or bracket to hold the battery.

You can check the scooter charging system by putting the scooter on its centre stand and connecting the voltage meter as described earlier. When you start the engine, the voltage meter should show a higher voltage as engine revs are increased, about 13.5-14.5 volts for a 12-volt system. If there's no change in the voltage, then the charging system needs expert examination, which is outside the scope of this handbook.

If you've followed all of the instructions in this section and battery condition has not improved, your only option will be to renew it.

SECTION H: Main fuse

In the event of electrical failure check the main (and only) fuse. It is normally located next to the battery. To access this, unclip the holder, open it up, remove the fuse and examine it. There is a thin filament of wire which runs from one end of the fuse to the other within a glass cylinder. If this filament is broken, the fuse is 'blown' and needs to be replaced with a new one of the correct rating, as stated in your scooter's handbook. You need to try and find the problem that caused the fuse to blow:

Fig 83. Typical glass fuses.

it will often be a burned-out bulb, or perhaps a loose live wire.

Caution! Using a fuse of a higher rating, or using wire or silver paper to bypass a blown fuse, can cause other electrical faults, or even a fire.

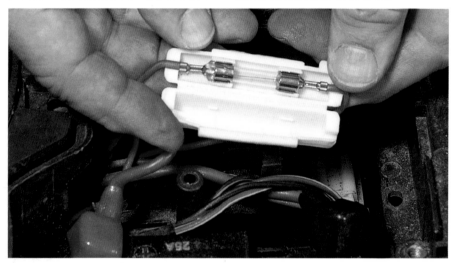

Fig 84. Fuse holder open showing main fuse.

SECTION I: Lights

Required:
Screwdriver

1: Headlight adjustment
Adjusting the main headlight is simply a matter of undoing the adjustment screw under the headlight, and pushing or pulling the headlight lens to alter its angle.

To obtain the correct headlight height adjustment, position the scooter approximately 9m (30ft) away from a 'screen' (such as a garage door). With the tyres at the correct pressure, sit on the machine, holding it upright in the riding position. Ask a helper to measure the height of the headlight bulb from the ground, and transfer this measurement onto the screen/garage door. Turn on the headlamp, using the main beam setting, and measure from the ground to the point between the illuminated area

on the screen and the dark area above. This point should be no more than 90 per cent and no less than 70 per cent of the main bulb height. For example, if the headlight bulb is 100cm above the ground, then the headlight beam should illuminate the area from ground level up to between 70cm and 90cm above the ground at a distance of 9m (30ft).

2: Changing bulbs
Required:
Bulbs
Socket set
Screwdrivers

Headlight
There are too many different styles of scooter on the market to describe each front light fitting individually. However, if the headlight is separate from the handlebar cowling, it's likely the light fitting will be held on by screws in the headlight rim, or, if the headlight is part

Fig 85. Headlamp beam adjuster (arrowed).

Fig 86. Typical bulbholder at rear of headlight fitting.

Fig 88. Replacing headlamp bulb in fitting.

Fig 87. Bulb in bulb holder.

of the handlebar cowling itself, then you will have to remove the cowling. The cowling will be fixed from underneath by screws or bolts.

Once you have removed the cowling, you should now be able to see the rear of the headlight unit.

Note: If the headlight bulb is a halogen bulb, try not to handle it by the glass, because it will discolour due to the natural oils of your skin.

There are two types of fitting.
1) Bayonet: Pull back the rubber cover to expose the holder. Twist the bulb holder to remove it from from the casing; the bulb is then removed by turning it anti-clockwise. Refitting is the reverse of removal.

2) Spring clip: If your scooter has the more modern spring fitting bulb holder, then disconnect the power feed cable from the back of the bulb. Push the sides of the springs inward to allow the spring to pivot away from the rear of the bulb. This will allow you to remove the bulb. Refitting is the reverse of removal.

Riding light

This is the light that is always on when you're riding. It may be fitted in the main light assembly, or as a separate item. If it's in the main fitting, removing it will be just a case of either a slight twist of the holder to release it, or, if a rubber mounting, a gentle pull to release it from the light assembly.

If the riding light is a separate unit, it will be a simple push-fit rubber mount,

Fig 89. Typical riding light (always on when riding).

Fig 90. Riding light bulb in holder.

or a small plastic mount which will require a slight twist to remove the bulb holder from the rear of the mounting.

Again, refitting is the reverse of removal.

Indicators (turn signal lights)

Access to the bulb in the case of front indicators is normally via a screw-secured lens. If the indicator lenses are not retained by screws, access to the bulbs is achieved by removing the back panel.

Rear indicators may be either separate from the rear light assembly, or part of it. If they're separate, the procedure for replacing the bulbs is the same as for the front indicators. If they're part of a single cluster incorporating the rear light, read on.

Rear light

There are three types of rear light assembly: the brake/stop light is included in the single assembly; the brake/stop light is a separate unit; and that which uses an LED (light emitting diode) light unit.

If the rear and brake/stop lights are in the same assembly, then access to the bulbs is simply a case of unscrewing

Fig 91. Removing typical indicator lens.

Fig 92. Lens removed, revealing bulb.

Fig 93. Typical single rear cluster.

Fig 95. Body panel removal.

Fig 94. Rear cluster with separate brakelight.

the light cover.

There are two types of rear brake/stop light assembly which are not built into the rear bulb unit. One is a separate body where simply unscrewing the light cover gives access to the bulbs. The other uses an LED light bulb unit.

This is a more complicated procedure to obtain access to the rear and indicator bulbs.

Typically the rear and indicator bulbs are accessed by first removing the numberplate, which gives you easy access to the small body panel below the light cluster and above the numberplate, behind which are the screws you need to access to remove the light cluster cover.

Fig 96. Easing off the rear light lens.

Fig 97. Rear light lens off, bulb revealed.

If access to the indicator bulbs is required, these covers are held by clips at the top and bottom. You'll need to gently squeeze them toward each other to get them to release. Refitting is the reverse of removal.

Separate LED brake/stop light unit
Required:
Spanners
Socket set
Screwdriver
Allen keys

To obtain access to the brake/stop light assembly, first open the seat compartment. The rear brake/stop light assembly can be part of a panel that incorporates the lifting handle, in which case both will have to be removed together.

Remove this small body panel.
Remove the two screws that secure the light cluster cover, which will then pull away, leaving the indicator covers in situ.

Undo the bolts that hold the lifting handle and rear brake/stop light assembly to the rear of the scooter. Disconnect the power feed to the light, making sure it doesn't slide back into its hole as retrieval would mean having to remove the main body panels.

Fig 98. Typical stop/brakelight unit.

Fig 99. Bolts securing lifting handle and brakelight assembly.

Turn the unit over and you will see that the brake/stop light unit is held in place by two screws. Undo these and the unit can be totally removed.

Note: This light unit is made up of small LEDs (light emitting diodes). They aren't individually renewable, so the whole unit will have to be replaced; but only if three or more 'bulbs' have blown. Don't forget to reconnect the power cable. Refitting is the reverse of removal, ensuring that the bolts which hold the lifting handle are tight.

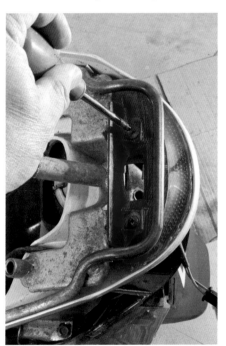

Fig 100. Underside of brakelight unit.

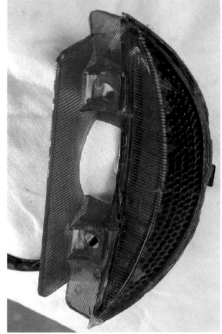

Fig 101. LED (light emitting diode) unit.

SECTION J: Tyres

Although the tyres require very little maintenance, they do need regular inspection. **Remember, your life depends on them!**
Look for:
Cuts in the treads and the tyre walls.
Bulges in the tyre walls.

You should also check the tyre tread with a proper tyre tread depth gauge; this is so that you can check the entire tyre circumference and not just where the wear indicators are.

Pay particular attention to the centre of the tread area of the tyre, and look for signs of the inner canvas showing through the tread where the tyre is extremely worn.

Fig 102. Tread depth indicators. When a tyre wears down level with any one of the minimum tread depth indicators (arrowed), it must be renewed.

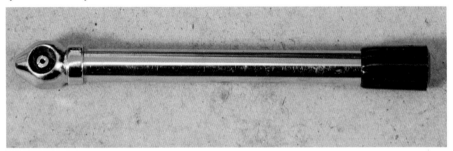

Fig 103. Analogue tyre pressure gauge (the black cap is a valve removal device).

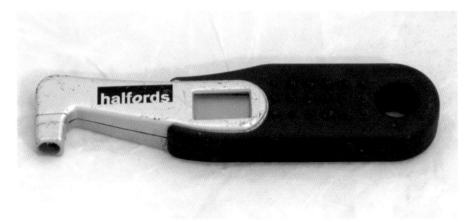

Fig 104. Digital tyre pressure gauge.

In the UK, at the time of writing, the minimum tyre tread depth was 1mm throughout a continuous band, measuring at least three-quarters of the breadth of the tread and round the entire outer circumference of the tyre, OR, if the grooves of the original tread pattern of the tyre do not extend beyond three-quarters of the breadth of the tread (ie, common with motorcycle tyres) any groove of the original pattern must have a minimum depth of at least 1mm.

Check the tyre pressure regularly with a tyre pressure gauge.

There are two types of tyre pressure gauge, analogue and digital.

To use a pressure gauge, first remove the dust cover from the tyre valve.

If using an analogue gauge, remove the black valve removal tool from the end of the gauge (if fitted).

Ensure that the extending part of the analogue gauge is fully inserted into the bodyshell.

Push the pressure gauge onto the tyre valve, and note that the end of the gauge will push out of the gauge casing. Remove the gauge from the valve, taking care not to move the extended end, and examine the readout point. Look for where a line under a number is level with the end of the gauge casing.

Fig 105. Tyre pressure readout here in psi (pounds per square inch).

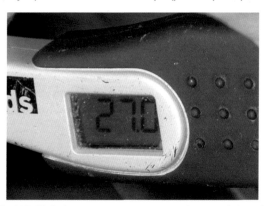

Fig 106. Digital tyre pressure gauge readout, again in psi.

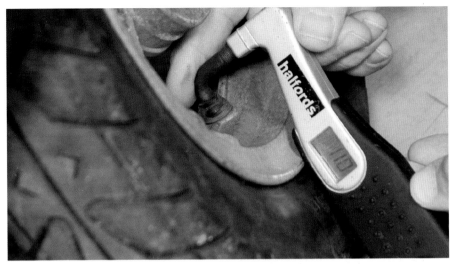

Fig 107. Digital tyre pressure gauge in use.

This number is the tyre pressure in your chosen unit of measurement (Fig 105).

If using a digital gauge (Fig 107), momentarily push the pressure gauge onto the tyre valve (some gauges bleep when they've recorded the pressure, others don't, in which case hold it on the valve for 3-5 seconds). Remove the gauge from the valve and read the tyre pressure from the display screen.

After checking the tyre pressure (and re-inflating, if necessary), replace the dust cover on the valve.

The size and type of tyre is indicated on the tyre wall. If the tyre needs renewal, it's important that the the tyre is replaced with one of the same size and type. Brand is not as important, although many consider a well known make is a better proposition than a cheaper brand.

Fig 108. Tyre size indicated on tyre wall.

Fig 109. Typical air filter box.

SECTION K: Air filter

1: Removal, examination and cleaning
Required:
Screwdriver
Socket set (for removal if required)
Small container of engine oil
Small container of petrol
Bowl

Do not run the engine without the air filter in place, as this could allow foreign bodies to get inside the engine and cause serious damage.

Wash the air filter box cover with clean, soapy water; this will prevent contaminating the filter when the cover is removed.

Undo all the screws or bolts holding the air filter box cover in place, and disconnect the air intake pipe.

Remove the air filter carefully – the sponge material is soft and easily torn. If the filter is backed by a paper element

Fig 110. Foam air filter element in position.

this will need to be renewed.

Examine the filter for cuts, rips or tears, and renew if there's any damage. If the filter is really dirty you'll need to clean it before refitting. Wash the filter in a bowl of warm soapy water, then rinse thoroughly with clean water. Gently squeeze out the excess fluid, but do not wring it out, and allow to dry.

Soak the filter in a proprietary air

Fig 111. Air filter housing with filter removed.

cleaner oil until the fluid has penetrated the filter. Carefully squeeze out any excess fluid, and allow the filter to dry thoroughly, before carefully refitting the filter into the filter box. Take care that any fittings which pass through the air filter are not trapped.

Check that the air filter is refitted correctly, particularly around the edges, then refit the filter box cover, checking that it's seated properly and all the fittings are correctly done up.

Ensure that the air filter intake pipe is fitted correctly, and the securing clip is fastened.

SECTION L: Body panels

1: Removal
Required:
Screwdrivers
Spanners
Socket set

It would be impossible to describe in detail every type of body panel. Suffice to say that if you need to remove any body panel for repair, take your time. All panels can be removed, but you'll need to look carefully at them to ascertain how they are held in position. There will be the obvious things, like screws and bolts, but also look for hidden clips and hooks, as in Fig 112, which would mean the two panels have to be slid along each other in order for them to come apart.

There should be no need to have to strain a joint for it to come apart.

2: Body panel repair
To repair a crack in a body panel, first remove the panel from the scooter.

Wash the panel with clean soapy water, rinse, and allow to dry thoroughly.

Clean the panel with a degreasing agent to remove all traces of grease or oil (which would prevent glue and/or paint adhering properly to the panel).

With the panel thoroughly cleaned, examine the crack and see how the edges mate together. If the crack is a straightforward one (ie, going in one direction across a flat surface), it can be repaired in one go with a fibreglass repair kit. If it traverses a number of bends or curves, then it's best to fibreglass it in sections, starting from the inside of the crack and then working outward toward the edge of the panel. Plan ahead with regard to how you're going to hold the cracked edges in place while the fibreglass sets. You can

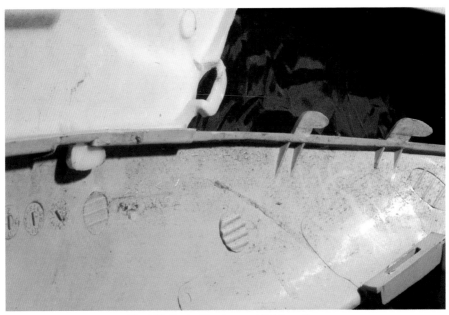

Fig 112. Typical body panel hidden clips.

Fig 113. Cracked panel needing repair.

Fig 114. Fibreglass mesh along back of crack.

Fig 115. Filled.

use pegs, clamps or tape, for example, or even make a former to help keep the joint together. Whichever way you intend to hold it in position, have a dry run first.

Mix the fibreglass resin as per the manufacturer's instructions, apply the resin to the mesh, and then apply the mesh to the inside of the panel over the crack, brushing down well and adding more resin if needed. Cover the crack by at least one inch each side. When the first section is dry, proceed to the next, making sure that it all lines up correctly. Continue until all sections are repaired and dry.

Now we need to prepare the exterior of the panel. I recommend that you rub down the paintwork by hand, and not use any electric sanding tools (they can run away from you, and they also generate a lot of heat which can cause problems with both the paint and the plastic). Using a fine grade wet and dry paper go over the entire panel to remove the lacquer and transfers covering the existing **paintwork**, using clean water to wash the dust away. As the panel is invariably plastic, you will get a better finish if, after repair, you respray the whole of the panel.

With any lacquer removed and the panel dry, using 180 grade wet and dry roughen around the crack on the outside of the panel to a distance of approximately two inches, to provide a key for the body filler.

Choose a filler that is suitable for use with plastics, filling all holes, cracks or ridges, and leaving the surface as close as possible to the correct profile. Try to keep the use of filler to a minimum as, once dry, it will take a lot of sanding to remove excess material. Using increasingly fine grades of wet and dry (down to 800 grade) on a sanding block, sand the filler until you have the correct shape and thickness, and the surface is smooth to the touch. Wash the panel three or four times using fresh clean water to make sure there's no dust on it, and allow it to dry thoroughly. Finally, wipe the panel with white spirit or turpentine.

Note: When spraying, a few thin coats will give a far better finish than one thick one. Spraying too close or too slowly will, in all likelihood, lead to runs in the paint; so practise first!

Spray the panel with a proprietary primer, working slowly from one end to the other, making sure you spray past the edges so as to keep the paint smooth. Maintain a steady movement and allow the paint to dry thoroughly between coats. Rub down with wet and dry (800 grade) again, wash the panel or wipe with white spirit, and allow to dry.

Repeat with another coat of primer and then rub down, wash and allow to dry again.

Now you can apply two coats of undercoat, in the same way as the primer, rubbing down between coats – using either a proprietary rubbing compound or very fine abrasive wet and dry paper (800 grade used wet).

Next, it's time to apply the top coat. Again, we apply two coats, but with no rubbing down between coats, unless required.

Finally, if you are happy with the appearance, and after you have applied any transfers/decals that are required, you can apply a coat of clear polyurethane lacquer to protect the new paintwork.

When all is dry, apply a coat of wax polish to protect the new paintwork.

Refit the panel to the scooter.

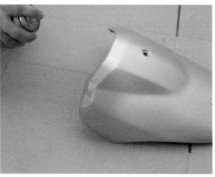

Fig 116. Applying primer.

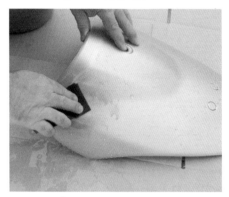

Fig 117. Rubbing down.

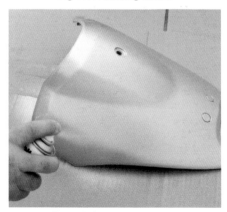

Fig 118. Applying top coat.

two
Drive safely

SECTION M: Cleaning your scooter

Required:
Hosepipe/large bucket
Soft brush
Shampoo
Sponge
Soft cloth
Polish/wax

If you use a hosepipe or power washer, do not direct the jet of water directly onto switches, electrical connections or (pressure washer only) tyres.

Wash the scooter with clean water and a soft brush to remove dirt, leaving the wheels until last. Wheels tend to accumulate grit, and you don't want this on the scooter body panels.

Caution! Don't use cleaners on the brake disc/s; they could seriously affect braking performance.

Now wash the scooter with a suitable automotive shampoo, using a soft sponge to wipe on and wipe off.

Do not 'drown' switches when washing because some types of shampoos contain 'wetting agents,' which would assist water penetration and could cause shorting of the electrical circuits. If you suspect water has got into electrical components, allow time for them to dry out thoroughly before use.

When the scooter is dry, polish it with a proprietary wax to help protect the paintwork.

Be aware that after a cleaning session the brakes will be wet, thereby increasing stopping distances until they have fully dried out.

SECTION N: Other safety checks

1: Checking the wheel bearings
Front wheel
With the front wheel raised off the ground, turn the handlebars fully to the left or right. With a helper holding the handlebars tightly at extreme lock, take hold of the wheel at the 3 o'clock and 9 o'clock positions.

Try to move the wheel by pushing one side and pulling the other, if you can feel any play, or hear a slight 'knock,' then the wheel bearings are loose and will need to be renewed (beyond the scope of this book).

Rear wheel
This check is performed in exactly the same way as the front wheel bearings, although due to access restrictions, you may have to hold the wheel in the 7 o'clock and 1 o'clock positions.

2: Checking swinging arm bearings
With the rear wheel off the ground, hold it where you can and, by rocking it toward and away from you, see if you can feel some sideways movement. If you can, the swinging arm bearing may need to be replaced (beyond the scope of this book).

Fig 119. Checking front wheel bearings.

Fig 120. Checking rear wheel bearings.

3: Steering head bearings

With the scooter off its stand, position yourself astride the machine, apply the front brake and try to move the scooter forward and backward; the scooter should go up and down on its suspension. If you can feel a slight 'knock' through the handlebars, then the steering head bearings may need to be changed, although, on some scooters these bearings can be adjusted. You can also test the bearings by putting the scooter on its centre stand, with the front wheel off

Fig 121. Checking steering head bearings.

Fig 122. Front suspension oil seals.

Fig 123. The rear suspension oil seal is inside the damper (the cylindrical object inside the spring).

the ground, push and pull gently on the bottom of the front forks to check for play. (Bearing renewal/adjustment is beyond the scope of this book.)

4: Suspension

Look for cracks in the oil seals, or oil leaks in and around the suspension. Any cracks or leaks will mean the oil seals have to be replaced, or, in the case of the rear suspension, a complete new suspension unit will have to be fitted (beyond the scope of this book). Also check for a cracked or broken rear spring.

three

Troubleshooting

Engine – poor performance	
Carburettor jet dirty or clogged	Clean or renew
Silencer blocked	Clean
Air filter dirty or clogged	Clean or renew
Fuel filter dirty or blocked	Clean or renew
Clutch slipping (engine accelerates but scooter does not pull away)	Refer to garage
Engine – hard to start	
Carburettor jet dirty or clogged	Clean or renew
Poor fuel delivery	Check inline fuel filter
	Check fuel in delivery pipe
	Check fuel
Air filter dirty or clogged	Clean
Engine flooded	Try to start engine with full throttle
	Remove and clean sparkplug to remove excess fuel
	Plug gap too big/small
Engine won't idle	
Incorrectly adjusted throttle	Re-adjust

Carburettor jet dirty	Clean jet
Water in carburettor	Refer to garage
Engine misfires	
Dirty/worn sparkplug	Clean or renew sparkplug
Dirty air filter	Clean or renew
Loose plug cap	Check for fit on plug
Wet plug cap	Allow to dry
High fuel consumption	
Clogged air filter	Clean or renew
Clutch mechanism slipping	Refer to garage
Scooter does not pull away	
Clutch faulty	Refer to garage
Clutch slipping	Refer to garage
Kickstart	
Pedal does not return	Check and grease, or renew the spring
Brakes	
Brakes make grinding noise	Check shoes and pads
Poor braking	Check shoes and pads
	Bleed brakes
No brakes	Check shoes and pads
	Check operation of levers and cables
	Check hydraulic fluid level/s
	Bleed brakes
Steering and suspension	
Steering wobbles	Wrong tyre pressure (inflate)
Excessive play in wheel bearings front and back	Refer to garage
Steering hard to turn	Refer to garage
Scooter bottoms out on suspension	Refer to garage
Battery/electrics	
Flat (discharged) battery	Charge
Battery flattens after each journey	Check output from charging circuit
No electrics	Check main fuse
No lights	Check main fuse/bulbs

four

Torque settings

Main torque wrench settings

	Nm	lb/ft	lb/in
Sparkplug	10-15	7-11	90-130
Exhaust mounting	30-36	22-27	260-319
Exhaust manifold nuts	10-14	7-10	89-124
Front wheel spindle nut	50-70	37-52	443-620
Rear wheel d/shaft nut	110-130	81-96	974-1150
Engine oil drain plug	10-15	7-11	89-133

Standard torque wrench settings

Where no torque wrench settings are specified, the settings below may be used as a guide. If the parts to be joined are not of a similar material, the torque setting may need to be reduced, ie in the case of a plastic panel bolting to a metal fitment.

	Nm	lb/ft	lb/in
M5 nut or bolt	5	4	44
M6 nut or bolt	10	7	89
M8 nut or bolt	21.5	16	190
M10 nut or bolt	35	26	310

Bolts with flanged head			
M6	12	9	106
M8	27	20	239
M10	40	30	354

Note: The nut or bolt size, for example M6, relates to the thread diameter, not the diameter of the head or nut.

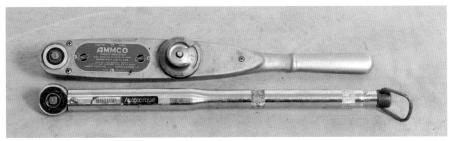

Fig 124. There are several types of torque wrenches available. Some click when a preset torque is reached, others have dials or readouts to show the torque being applied. They may be a little more expensive than other hand tools, but can prevent dangerous/expensive tightening mistakes.

five

Resources

Magazines
Twist & Go.

Scootering Magazine
The UK's biggest scootering magazine
– over 130 pages of features, reviews,
events and classifieds.

Classic Scooterist Scene
A bi-monthly magazine dedicated to
both the classic and modern scooterist.

Motor Cycle Monthly
A free national motorcycle newspaper;
written by enthusiasts *for* enthusiasts.

Importers/dealers
The following importers will be able to direct you to your local dealership.

Brand	Telephone	Website
Adly	01543 466789	www.adly.co.uk
Aprilia	0208 290 8800	www.aprilia.com
Baotian	01227 720700	www.baotianuk.com
Barossa	01539 536655	www.astrogeneral.com
Benelli	0844 412 8450	www.benelli.co.uk
CF Moto	01455 292 688	www.ecoscooters.co.uk
CPI	01226 284466	www.cpimoto.co.uk (parts only)
Daelim	0844 412 8450	www.daelim.co.uk
Derbi	0844 801 0752	www.derbi.com

Brand	Telephone	Website
E-Max	0207 209 5371	www.e-transportgroup.com
Generic	01869 363636	www.genericmotors.co.uk
Gilera	0844 801 0752	www.gilera.com
Honda	0845 200 8000	www.honda.co.uk
Hyosung	01869 363636	www.hyosung.co.uk
Keeway	0844 412 8450	www.keewaymotor.co.uk
KYMCO	01743 761107	www.kymco.co.uk
Lexmoto	0845 459 2369	www.lexmoto.co.uk
LML	01384 480490	www.lmlscooter.co.uk
Peugeot	01202 810200	www.peugeotscooters.co.uk
PGO	01869 363636	www.pgoscooters.co.uk
Piaggio	0208 290 8800	www.piaggio.com
Pulse	0845 459 2369	www.pulsemoto.co.uk
Rieju	01526 834357	www.riejumoto.com
Sachs	01202 823344	www.sachbikes.co.uk
Suzuki	0500 011 959	www.suzuki.co.uk
Sym	01332 274260	www.symscooters.co.uk
TGB	01539 536655	www.tgbmotors.co.uk
Vespa	00800 818 29800	www.vespa.com
Wuyang	01728 833020	www.davidsilverspares.co.uk
Yamaha	01932 358121	www.yamaha-motor.co.uk
ZingBikes	0845 555 1234	www.zingbikes.com

ISBN: 978-1-845841-02-7
Paperback • 15x10.5cm • £4.99* UK/$9.95* USA
• 208 pages • 200 colour pictures

For more info on Hubble & Hattie titles, visit our website at
www.hubbleandhattie.com
• email: info@hubbleandhattie.com
• Tel: +44(0)1305 260068
* prices subject to change, p&p extra

Also from Veloce Publishing –

ISBN: 978-1-845843-51-9
Paperback • 21x14.8cm • £9.99*
UK/$19.95* USA • 96 pages • 32
colour pictures

For more info on Veloce titles, visit our
website at www.veloce.co.uk • email:
info@veloce.co.uk • Tel: +44(0)1305
260068
* prices subject to change, p&p extra

ISBN: 978-1-845843-10-6
Paperback • 21x14.8cm • £12.99*
UK/$24.95* USA • 128 pages • 67
colour and b&w pictures

For more info on Veloce titles, visit our
website at www.veloce.co.uk • email:
info@veloce.co.uk • Tel: +44(0)1305
260068
* prices subject to change, p&p extra

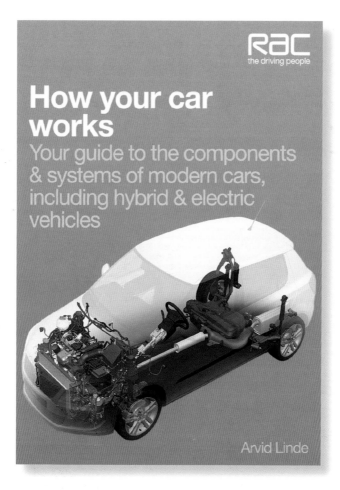

ISBN: 978-1-845843-90-8
Paperback • 21x14.8cm • £12.99* UK/$24.95* USA
• 128 pages • 92 colour and b&w pictures

For more info on Veloce titles, visit our website at www.veloce.
co.uk • email: info@veloce.co.uk • Tel: +44(0)1305 260068
* prices subject to change, p&p extra

Also from Veloce Publishing –

ISBN: 978-1-845843-88-5
Paperback • 21x14.8cm • £9.99*
UK/$19.95* USA • 80 pages • 110
pictures

For more info on Veloce titles, visit our
website at www.veloce.co.uk • email:
info@veloce.co.uk • Tel: +44(0)1305
260068
* prices subject to change, p&p extra

ISBN: 978-1-845843-96-0
Paperback • 21x14.8cm • £9.99*
UK/$19.95* USA • 96 pages • 209
colour pictures

For more info on Veloce titles, visit our
website at www.veloce.co.uk • email:
info@veloce.co.uk • Tel: +44(0)1305
260068
* prices subject to change, p&p extra

Index

VISIT VELOCE ON THE WEB – WWW.VELOCE.CO.UK
All current books • New book news • Special offers • Gift vouchers • Forum